COCKINGTON GREEN GARDENS
a work of art

As captured in the paintings of
Isla Patterson

echo))
BOOKS

Published in 2024 by Echo Books.

Echo Books is an imprint of Superscript Publishing Pty Ltd, ABN 76 644 812 395

Registered Office: Registered Office: PO Box 669, Woodend, Victoria, 3442.

www.echobooks.com.au

Copyright ©The Trustee for the Cockington Green Family Trust

Creator: Miller, John, Author

Title: Cockington Green Gardens : A work of Art

ISBN: 978-1-922603-62-3

Book layout and design by Peter Gamble, Canberra
Set in Helvetica Neue-Thin, 11/16, and
MinervaModern.

able of Contents

Table of Contents continued

Introduction

First opened on 3rd November 1979, Cockington Green Gardens has become one of Canberra's best-loved and most iconic tourist attractions. Building on site commenced in 1976.

The attraction's genesis dates back to 1972, when Doug and Brenda Sarah and their three young children, Mark, Sally-Anne, and Melinda, set off on an extended holiday to the United Kingdom. This trip was a long-awaited return to Brenda's country of birth after she arrived in Australia with her mother, father, and sister in 1952.

Doug, Brenda, and their children visited many places during their UK odyssey. One of those places was Babbacombe, near Torquay in the south-western English county of Devon. Babbacombe was home to a model village established by Tom Dobbins in 1963. With a building background and an acute eye for detail, Doug was immediately impressed by what he saw. He and Brenda also had a strong interest in gardens, a significant feature of Babbacombe Model Village.

That visit was indelibly etched in their memories as they travelled around the UK for most of 1972. It catalysed their ultimate decision to develop Cockington Green Gardens in Canberra.

The attraction was originally a display of model buildings from Great Britain. Around 20 years after opening, the attraction expanded to include buildings from around the world. Many of the new buildings were undertaken with support from Embassies and High Commissions of different countries with representation in Australia.

A feature of the attraction has been the immaculate landscaped gardens, which provide a perfect backdrop for the many different scenes.

As the attraction continued to develop and expand, contact was made with well-known local artist Isla Patterson. Isla was a member of a group of artists known as Art in Miniature. The approach was to determine Isla's interest in painting various scenes at Cockington Green Gardens, most notably the international buildings. Following an agreement with Isla to reproduce the buildings in the art form, the relationship between Isla and Doug and Brenda Sarah led to the commercial sale of Isla's artworks at Cockington Green Gardens. This arrangement continues today.

This publication has been designed to capture Isla's beautiful artworks as she has interpreted the fantastic detail and works of Doug and Brenda's models as set in various parts of this award-winning attraction.

About
Isla Patterson

Isla was born in South Australia and took up art in the late 1960s. She studied art in South Aust with Trevor Clare and watercolours with Ruth Tuck. Isla lived in the USA from 1975 to 1978, where continued her art studies, belonged to the International Art Society, and held her first solo exhibitio

Isla's work has been recognized across Australia, winning many watercolour and painting award numerous shows and exhibitions in metropolitan, regional and rural centres. Isla has held more t 20 successful solo exhibitions and has paintings in private and public collections throughout Aust and overseas.

Besides Isla's significant body of work over many years, her contribution to the art world has included teaching and judging at exhibitions. Her contribution also included setting up and conduc classes and exhibitions for the Multiple Sclerosis Society of the ACT.

In addition to producing the watercolours of many of Cockington Green Gardens' model buildings, has been commissioned for other commercial projects and private work.

Canberra, as home to High Commissions and Embassies of countries represented in Austr inspired the book titled *International Treasures: Canberra's Embassies*. The book, authored by Dorc Hart, features Isla's paintings of some of the unique embassy and high commission building Canberra's diplomatic area. The book was published in 2017 and launched at the National Librar Australia on 27th September 2017. It included a foreword by former Governor General, Major Ger the Hon Michael Jeffrey AC, AO(Mil), CVO, MC (Ret'd).

In addition to her superb watercolours of the model buildings commissioned by Cockington Gr Gardens, held in a private collection, Isla has produced other works, including Australian birds, wild and landscapes, displayed in Cockington Green Gardens' Rose Room.

oreword

Over the past two decades, we have built a business association and a wonderful friendship with Isla Patterson. As admirers of original artworks of Australian wildlife and landscapes, we were immediately captured by the style, colour, and detail of Isla's paintings when visiting one of her stand-alone exhibitions.

We then approached Isla with a proposition to consider applying her considerable skills to replicate our models in art. We both agreed that Isla possessed the skills and qualities to bring the models to life and add a third dimension to the original buildings and structures. Having some lovely artwork, ultimately created by Isla, also opened up other opportunities, including this book.

Isla has an incredible eye for detail. We are thrilled with how she has been able to pick up minute details from our buildings and translate them into lovely artwork. We believe this will provide lots of enjoyment for others. It is such a wonderful gift when you can see something and recreate it on canvas or some other medium, becoming a replication and a thing of beauty that can often take on different meanings.

Isla's reputation as a quality artist is quickly confirmed when you see all the awards she has received. Recognition has also been bestowed on her by her peers and others who purchased her works or commissioned Isla for specific projects. It is a tribute to Isla to know that her artworks can be found in Australia and other countries. We feel very privileged to know Isla and understand her devotion to producing quality work that many admire.

We are confident that this book will provide you with many fond memories of your visit to Cockington Green Gardens or any of the original buildings or structures included in these pages. Our heartfelt thanks go to Isla for collaborating on this book and for the years of friendship we have thoroughly enjoyed.

Doug & Brenda Sarah
Founders, Creators and Owners
Cockington Green Gardens

September 2024

The Original Display

Isla Patterson's re-creation of the main building's facade, captured from inside the attraction, features in the foreground some of the models from the village of Cockington, where the attraction's name has its origins.

The main building has become an iconic landmark. Doug Sarah constructed it with his father-in-law, Bill Rose, and occasional support from specialised trades. It took around two and a half years to build, and its roof pitch is 50 degrees.

Isla has superbly framed this aspect of the main building to reflect the serenity and scale of the display and highlight its detail. The main building includes the attraction's main entry, souvenir shop, and administrative office.

Main Buildin

la Patterson

This painting by Isla Patterson beautifully depicts the peacefulness of Cockington Green Gardens. The waterfall scene is in the original area of the display and was installed to bring the calmness of water and colour into the attraction. The topography of the landscape feeds a nearby stream and pond.

This particular work by Isla also brings together the concept of a changing season with the harmony of sound and moving water to tease the imagination of anyone viewing the painting.

Waterfall

The inspiration for Cockington Green Gardens was from a family visit to the United Kingdom in the early 1970s. During that visit, the family came across the quaint village of Cockington in Torquay, Devon. The original thatched village of Cockington, as reproduced by Isla from the Cockington Green Gardens display, sits at the entrance to Cockington Country Park. This highly visited but protected landmark area includes the historic Cockington Court manor.

Cockington Country Park was owned only by three families between 1066 and 1932 before passing into public ownership. These are some of the very early models built by Doug Sarah in the late 1970s before the attraction's opening in November 1979.

Cockington Village, Devon

Isla Patterson

Isla perfectly captures the majesty of Braemar Castle in this painting. The Royal Standard waving in the breeze and the gated entrance provide an insight into the importance of this structure. Braemar in Scotland was near the heart of the late Queen Elizabeth II, as she was patron of the Braemar Royal Highland Society and missed the annual Braemar Gathering only four times in 70 years.

Even at one-twelfth scale, the Braemar Castle miniature building is very prominent within the Cockington Green Gardens display. This was another model made by Doug Sarah before the opening of Cockington Green Gardens in 1979, as were each of the models in the original display of buildings from Great Britain.

Braemar Castle,
Scotland

Isla Patterson

Original Queen Anne facade buildings date back to the early 18th century in recognition of Queen Anne, who reigned from 1702 to 1714. The painting produced by Isla is cleverly in keeping with most Queen Anne façade buildings, which are more like manor homes than the stately buildings of nobles.

The model in the grounds at Cockington Green Gardens, built by Doug Sarah in the 1970s, is a replica of a manor house found in Lewes, which is located in East Sussex, where the home of Henry XIII's fourth wife, Anne of Cleves can be found.

Queen Anne Facade, East Sussex

Isla Patterson

Isla Patterson

The Ferry Inn, Norfolk

The Ferry Inn at Horning in Norfolk has a tranquil, relaxing waterside setting and a colourful past. It suffered damage during a Luftwaffe bombing raid on 26 April 1941 and sustained significant damage when its then-thatched roof caught fire in 1965.

Isla Patterson captures the peaceful setting in her painting, including the building with its original thatched roof, which has since been replaced with a slate roof.

The Fitzwilliam Arms Hotel in Peterborough, north of London, is typical in design and structure of traditional English pubs dotted throughout the country. These pubs add much to the culture and landscape of rural and regional England. This pub is special to Cockington Green Gardens' founder, Brenda Sarah, with Peterborough being home to much of Brenda's family for many years.

Isla has nicely used a quiet surrounding landscape to gain the external solitude of such an important community social setting, but with a sense of mystery about the noise and hilarity of local patrons gathered inside.

Fitzwilliam Arms Hotel, Cambridgeshire

la Patterson

The historic Roman town of Godmanchester in Cambridgeshire has many listed buildings. The Godmanchester shops scene at Cockington Green Gardens includes a small selection of interesting buildings on the Causeway that runs along the river. The building's origins date back to the 16th and 17th centuries.

Isla's artistic interpretation of the model set within the grounds of Cockington Green Gardens beautifully captures the tranquility of England's small villages and countryside.

Godmanchester Shops, Cambridgeshire

Isla Petterson

Isla Patterson

Duxford Mill, Cambridgeshire

Duxford Mill is located in Duxford, Cambridgeshire, just south of the historic city of Cambridge. Its origins date back to the 18th century. The building underwent rebuilding in the early 19th century, and further modifications were made in the late 19th century. It wasn't until around 1946 that architect H.C. Hughes restored it and converted it into a residential property.

An interesting fact about this building is that the model at Cockington Green Gardens needed to be rebuilt after discovering that the original model was mirror-reversed due to the images used in its reproduction.

Isla has majestically created the peacefulness and beauty that are immediately apparent when viewing the grounds surrounding the original building.

Village Church

The village church has long been synonymous with life in the English countryside. Alongside the many magnificent and historic cathedrals throughout the United Kingdom, quaint churches are either at the heart of the many beautiful towns and villages or just on the outskirts in picturesque and peaceful settings.

The Cockington Green Gardens village church scene is a simple setting with a wedding taking place. Isla's painting brings life to that wedding scene, which takes place alongside the old graveyard and is also a feature of many church settings

Isla Patterson

The House in the Clouds, built in 1923, is a repurposed water tower in Thorpeness, Suffolk, which was built to receive water pumped from nearby Thorpeness Windmill. It was designed to improve the look of the water tower, disguising its tank with the appearance of a weatherboarded building that is more in keeping with Thorpeness's mock Tudor and Jacobean style. The original capacity of the water tank was 50,000 imperial gallons (230,000 L), but during the Second World War, the House in the Clouds was hit by gunfire from anti-aircraft guns based at Thorpeness.

In 1977, the village's main water supply made the water tower redundant, creating additional living space. In 1979, the main water tank was removed to convert the building into a house fully. The building now has five bedrooms and three bathrooms; it includes 85 steps from top to bottom and is around 70 ft (21 m) high.

With tulips in the foreground of Isla's depiction of the House in the Clouds display, a distinctly Dutch flavour is associated with this very English scene

The House
in the Clouds,
Suffolk

Isla Patterson

The International Display

The Borgund Stave Church from Borgund, Lærdel, Norway, took Doug Sarah more than 1,500 hours to construct before its placement in Cockington Green Gardens' international area. This fascinating building is built to a scale of 1:18.

Built between 1180 and 1250 A.D., Borgund Stave Church is classified as a triple nave stave church. It is no longer used for regular church functions but is now operated as a museum by the Society for the Preservation of Ancient Norwegian Monuments. The stave church name originates from the walls formed by vertical wooden boards or staves.

Isla's majestic painting of this unique structure captures in fantastic detail the four carved dragons' heads swooping from the carved ridge roof crests.

Borgund Stave Church, Norway

Borobudur Temple, Indonesia

Borobudur Temple in Indonesia was one of the few models in the display that were not constructed at Cockington Green Gardens. This highly recognized and significant temple is the largest Buddhist monument in the world, and the replica was made by two amazing Indonesian artisans, Mr. Wahyu Indrasan and Mr. Lukito.

Isla's painting carefully reproduces the sculpting's detail and intricacy, which is embedded into this wonderous structure.

The village of Hollókő in Hungary is so significant that it is included on the UNESCO World Heritage Register. The village was developed mainly in the 18th and 19th centuries, although it has been the subject of considerable destruction and reconstruction over the centuries. The village reflects rural life before the 20th-century agricultural revolution. Nowadays, the old national traditions of Hollókő come to life each Easter when villagers wear national costumes for two days while enjoying festivities.

Through her painting, Isla has beautifully captured the serenity of this restored village, which holds much sentiment and history for the people of Hungary. Roland Schmitz took around 750 hours to construct this replica carefully.

Hollókö, Hungar

Isla Patterson

Dabotap Pagoda and Seokgatap Pagoda, both built around 751 A.D., are the two most famous features of the World Heritage Listed Bulguksa Temple located on the slopes of Mt. Toham, South Korea's No. 1 Historic and Scenic site. The Pagodas are considered the most excellent specimens with their complex and ingenious architecture and 'profound philosophical depth and aesthetic charm.' The site includes the 9.17m tall Cheomseongdae Astronomical Observatory, constructed in the 7th century under the reign of Queen Seondeok. It is the oldest surviving astronomical observatory in Asia and possibly the world.

Isla's watercolour exquisitely projects the importance and visual calmness of these historical and culturally significant structures, which have stood for more than 1,200 years. Mark Sarah and Rob Pavlekovic constructed the Cockington Green Gardens models in 2006, which required around 1,200 hours to complete.

Dabotap Pagoda, Seokgatap Pagoda, and Bulguksa Temple, South Korea

Machu Picchu, Peru

Machu Picchu, built in the 15th century, is one of the world's most recognisable historical sites and is considered one of the Seven New Wonders of the World. It is widely believed that Inca royalty, high priests, and others retreated to Machu Picchu upon the arrival of the Spanish conquistadors led by Francisco Pizzaro in the early 1530s.

This modern-day wonder was said to have only been occupied for around 80 years before being abandoned and then rediscovered more than 300 years later by Yale University historian Hiram Bingham in 1911. The abandonment of Machu Picchu is also a mystery, although lack of water is cited as one of the reasons for its demise.

Machu Picchu's site at 7,710 feet above sea level is cleverly reflected in Isla's painting. Sharp peaks in the background and skies provide a colder and threatening feel that often comes with elevation. Doug Sarah, Mark Sarah, and Rob Pavlekovic collaborated for almost 2,500 hours to complete this complex model.

Château de Bojnice is one of Slovakia's most visited attractions and was first mentioned in written records in 1013, although construction is said to have commenced in the 12th century. It began as a wooden fort but was gradually replaced by stone, with the outer walls said to match the uneven, rocky terrain where the building was sited. The Château has had numerous owners and occupiers during its lengthy history, including Czech entrepreneur Jan Antonín Baťa, owner of the Bata shoe company. Bata acquired the property in February 1939. The Czechoslovak government confiscated the property in 1945 when it became home to various state institutions.

Australian and Slovakian ties are very strong. On 26 January 1949, Jan Jandura, a Slovakian, was the first person to be naturalised under the Australian Citizenship Program. A park in O'Connor in the ACT is named after Mr Jandura to commemorate this significant event.

Isla creates incredible depth and scale in her reproduction of this magnificent structure, which Doug Sarah and Rob Pavlekovic took around 2,000 hours to replicate.

Château de Bojnic
Slovak

Isla Patterson

El Caminito means "little walkway" or "little path" in Spanish. The display of Caminito is a thriving and lively street museum and traditional alleyway in La Boca, a well-known neighbourhood of the Argentinian capital of Buenos Aries.

Like many places with a romantic aura or nostalgic flavour, Caminito began in lesser splendour as a bridge over a tiny stream before becoming an abandoned railway area and, subsequently, a dump. Artist Benito Quinquela Martin is credited with Caminito's restoration from his paintings of the rough port life around La Boca.

There is an irony in that an area that owes its current form and existence to an artist is now on display in the miniature form a world away in Australia and recaptured in this vibrant piece by another artist, Isla Patterson. Roland Schmitz worked for around 1,000 hours to complete the models for this display.

El Caminito
La Boc

Isla Patterson

Like much of Latin America, Chile's architecture is in the Spanish Colonial style, mainly reflected in properties such as Casa Vega, a typical countryside property in central Chile.

The Casa Vega property is a 19th-century building with one-metre-thick walls and interconnecting rooms. The covered veranda encapsulating this rectangular homestead on each side is a feature of many rural homes of this period.

Isla's watercolour captures both the simplicity of the architecture and building and its contrast with the often-dry landscape upon which these buildings were set. Doug Sarah was assisted in constructing this model by Dominique Tarud and Gabriela Steger, who accompanied their husbands on their Australian diplomatic postings. The model required around 650 hours of work to complete.

Casa Vega, Chile

Iola Patterson

El Capitolio was included as a Venezuelan National Historical Monument on 22nd August 1992. It was built in 1872, adopted a radically anticlerical design, and introduced contemporary architecture to Caracas. The building has its own Oval Room, an elliptically shaped room crowned by a gilded oval-shaped dome. The dome's ceiling has paintings that vividly depict the defining Battle of Carabobo and the Venezuelan War of Independence against Spanish colonial rule.

El Capitolio, formerly occupied by Convent Nuns of Conception, is built in a neoclassical style with Doric and Corinthian columns. The Oval Room contains the proceedings of the Constitutional Congress (1811-12), including a handwritten version of the Declaration of Independence of Venezuela.

The colouring used by Isla as both a backdrop to the building and in framing the foreground sets a scene of vibrancy renowned throughout South America, including Venezuela. Roland Schmitz took over 900 hours to complete this very ornate model.

El Capitolio, Venezuela

Isla Patterson

The windmills of the La Mancha region will be forever part of history because of the work of one of the world's most famous and pre-eminent novelists, Miguel de Cervantes. It was the windmill setting in Cervantes' great novel, *El Ingenioso Hidalgo Don Quijote de la Mancha* (or simply Don Quixote), where Quixote was warned by his companion that his enemies were indeed not giants but windmills.

The windmills of the historic town of Consuegra, with its 12th-century castle, have become a revered part of the Castilla-La Mancha windmill trail and provide a perfect window into Miguel de Cervantes' great 17th-century novel.

Isla has cleverly embedded the figure of Don Quixote jousting with the "giant" windmill reproduced in miniature at Cockington Green Gardens. The model windmills (five on display) took Doug Sarah around 500 hours to construct.

Windmills of
La Mancha region,
Spain

Château Le Réduit, or The State House, is today the official residence of the President of Mauritius. It was initially constructed in 1748-49 by the Governor of the Isle de France, Pierre Félix Barthelemy David, as a fortress to defend attackers during a rivalry between the French and the English for colonial possessions in the Indian Ocean.

From around 1764, Château Le Réduit served as the residence of Governors of Mauritius, both French and British. The property was subject to many modifications from 1764 to 1778. The British took control of the island in 1810, and further changes and repairs to the building were undertaken. Leading botanists also paid significant attention to the grounds.

Isla has blended the building and landscape elements to give her watercolour an authentic colonial flavour. Colonialism is a feature of countries such as Mauritius. Roland Schmitz dedicated 1,200 hours between mid-2006 and 2007 to recreating Château Le Réduit.

Château Le Réduit, Mauritius

Sala Patterson

Groot Constantia is South Africa's oldest wine estate, dating back to 1685 when the land was first granted to Simon van der Stel, the last Commander and first Governor of the Cape Colony, the Dutch settlement at South Africa's Cape of Good Hope.

Van der Stel then built the classic Cape Dutch-style manor house and began to use the land to grow vines for wine production, other fruits and vegetables, and farming cattle. Van der Stel's original estate was broken into three parts following his death in 1712, and Groot Constantia continued to expand and develop as a wine estate under the ownership of the Cloete family until 1885. The estate was famous for its production of the Constantia dessert wine. The manor house was destroyed by fire in 1925 and was subsequently fully reconstructed to its original Cape Dutch splendour from funds raised.

Isla's watercolour uses sunlight and landscape settings to build the imagination about early life around Groot Constantia, long before today's landscape was developed. This was one of the first buildings completed for the new International Area at Cockington Green Gardens and took Doug Sarah over 450 hours to complete.

Groot Constantia,
South Africa

Lila Patterson

Slovenia is a country of incredible beauty with properties of diverse architectural styles reflecting the differing aspects of Slovenian culture, geography, and socio-economic background. Liznjek House, dating back to 1796, was the wealthiest homestead in Kranjska Gora, with 84 hectares of land. Dominko Homestead is an L-shaped building with a thatched roof. It is the oldest preserved homestead of the Pannonian style at around 300 years old. Divaca, a small town in the Slovene Karst region, is home to Skratelj's homestead and has a rich architectural style.

Isla's painting of the Slovenian homestead depicts the gentleness and serenity of a quiet lifestyle found in this exquisite country. Rob Pavlekovic and Mark Sarah devoted around 1,000 hours to creating the model on display at Cockington Green Gardens.

Liznjek House,
Slovenia

Isla Patterson

Karlštejn Castle was founded in 1348 by Charles IV, German king and King of Bohemia (1346-1378) and Holy Roman Emperor (1355-1378), to protect the imperial crown jewellery and the symbol of the crown of Bohemia.

Today, Karlstejn Castle is one of the most popular destinations in the Czech Republic after Prague. This classic medieval castle was completed some 20 years after construction, with Charles IV supervising construction and interior design.

Isla's ability to use space and colour ensures that the scale and prominence of the building are perfectly captured in her beautiful painting. Replicating this detailed building into a model at Cockington Green Gardens took Doug Sarah and Rob Pavlekovic over 2,000 hours.

Karlštejn Castle,
Czech Republic

Trakai Castle, Lithuania

Situated on Galvé Lake, Lithuania, construction of the Island Castle began in the second half of the 14th century by Grand Duke Kęstusis and was concluded in the early 15th century by his son, Vytautas. Built as a fortress, raiders never conquered the Island Castle, and thus, its purpose was achieved.

As with many historical sites throughout the centuries, the structure has been subject to considerable damage and decay. Serving as a prison and then suffering damage during the 17th-century wars with Muscovy, the decay of the Castle escalated, and it gradually fell into disrepair. Major reconstruction, repair, and conservation occurred following World War II, returning Trakai Castle to a 15th-century style.

Galvé Lake's tranquillity and the Island Castle's majesty perfectly blend into the lovely Isla Patterson watercolour. Mindaugas Mauragis made the model one of the few not built by Cockington Green Gardens model makers.

This Georgian-style Treaty House has a rich and controversial history, even preceding its construction in 1833-34 for the British Resident in New Zealand, James Busby. The New South Wales governor considered the property's original design by John Verge too extravagant, and it was subsequently halved in size following the intervention of colonial architect Ambrose Hallen.

The grounds of the Treaty House in various forms bear witness to the signing of two of New Zealand's most significant documents, the Declaration of Independence of New Zealand in 1835 and the Treaty of Waitangi in 1840. The Treaty of Waitangi, the founding bi-cultural document of New Zealand, was signed by northern Maori Chiefs and Captain William Hobson, representing Queen Victoria of Great Britain.

Isla has given importance to this historic building through elevation in her watercolour portrayal of Treaty House, which Roland Schmitz spent around 600 hours in 2006 creating as a model replica.

Treaty House, Waitangi, New Zealand

Isla Patterson

Al-Khazneh, Jordan

Petra in Jordan is one of the world's great historical sites, with centuries of incredible human habitation and creation stories. Confirmation of its great importance is found in UNESCO's description of the ancient city as "one of the most precious cultural properties of man's cultural heritage". Al Khazneh is Petra's most famous edifice whose function during Nabataean times remains unknown mainly, although believed to have been the mausoleum of the Nabatean King, Aretas IV Philopatris, in the 1st century AD.

Carved out of sandstone rockface, the structure is some 50 metres high and 30 metres wide and is seen as one of the most elegant remains of antiquity. Although its persona is vast, the interior is surprisingly small.

This beautiful painting replication by Isla Patterson of the model at Cockington Green Gardens is laced with incredible detail and texture, bringing life to the site. Rob Pavlekovic and Mark Sarah replicated this historical site for Cockington Green Gardens in 2006, taking over 1,000 hours to complete the project.

Isla Patterson

Tenochtitlan, Mexico

Founded on 20 June 1325, Tenochtitlan was a city-state in the centre of Mexico City. It was the spiritual and physical heart and capital of the expanding Aztec empire until it was captured by the Spanish in 1521.

The enormous pyramid of Templo Mayor, the main temple of Tenochtitlan that served as the base for the twin temples of Tláloc and Huitzilopochtli, was outstanding in size. It had a double stairway flanked on either side by low-solid balustrades. The Aztec history was one of integration and rejection until they finally found an omen that indicated where they should settle indefinitely, that omen being an eagle devouring a serpent on top of a cactus. In that spot, they founded their capital, Mexico-Tenochtitlan, in 1325 A.D.

The massive reflective pool on which Templo Mayor sat gave Ilsa a perfect setting to mirror her original watercolour. Doug Sarah, with the assistance of Gabriela Steger and Dominique Tarud, took around 1,000 hours to complete the model on display at Cockington Green Gardens.

Isla Patterson

Turkey's Kiz Kulesi (Leander's Tower) story is one of complexity and historical debate, laden with mystery and mythology. The Tower's history dates back some 2,500 years from its early beginnings when Athenian commander Alkibiades built a small tower in 411 B.C. to control the passage of boats from the Bosphorus. Beyond that, the first specific structure of the tower today occurred during the 12th century under the reign of Roman Emperor Manuel I Komnenos.

During the Ottoman Empire, the tower was further transformed for military purposes and continued to be reconstructed and repaired after various damage and destruction from fire and earthquake. It has since served as a quarantine station, a lighthouse, and now a café and an exclusive restaurant in the evening.

Isla's painting captures the isolation of the Tower, which was designed to act as a control station for vessels and later a fortress for the military. Rob Pavlekovic and Mark Sarah collaborated for over 1,100 hours to complete the model on display at Cockington Green Gardens.

Leander's Tower,
Turkey

With over 1,000 windmills in the Holland region today, the windmill is unquestionably the one thing that would cross the minds of most when thinking about this fascinating part of the Netherlands, a country with so much history and tradition. The low-lying lands of the Holland region made it necessary to find a way to ensure that water could be removed from the lowlands and back into the rivers and dikes to allow land to be farmed.

The Binnenkruier Windmill was a variation of the standard windmill in that the sails could be turned into the wind with a mechanism. One such windmill is the Mill De Twiskemolen (Twisk-mill) in the principality of Landsmeer in North Holland.

This Isla Patterson recreation features the detail in the windmill sails and the heavily timbered structure of the building. Peter Spronson constructed the Binnenkruier Windmill at Cockington Green Gardens.

Binnenkruier Windmill, Netherlands

St. Mark's Church was built around the end of the 12th or early 13th Centuries. It was built in the centre of an old secular settlement that was granted the privileges of a "Free Royal Town" in 1242 following the withdrawal of the Mongols.

The building, with its Late Gothic style and Romanesque features, has undergone several changes, with significant reconstruction reported around the late 14th Century. The striking tiled roof featuring the emblem of Zagreb on the right-hand side and the medieval coat of arms of Croatia, Slavonia, and Dalmatia on the left-hand side was constructed in 1880.

Isla has captured the intricacy associated with the incredible tiling on the roof. Over three thousand individual tiles were laid on the model constructed by Rob Pavlekovic, who is of Croatian heritage. The entire model took around 2,000 hours to create, giving some insight into the level of detail given to the models found at Cockington Green Gardens.

St. Mark´s Church,
Croatia

Sola Patterson.

St. Andrij Church, Ukraine

St. Andrij Church in Kyiv, Ukraine, is a Baroque-style architectural masterpiece by Italian architect Bartolomeo Rastrelli and a cultural heritage landmark. The church, also known as a cathedral, was constructed between 1747 and 1754 and sits atop a steep hill, which today is challenging preservationists because of notable shifts in the structure's foundations.

Isla had beautifully recreated the grandeur of this historic church, which began in the first century A.D. when Saint Andrew was said to have placed a cross in the ground on the site where the church now sits. St. Andrij Church is one of four architectural national treasures of Ukraine, as listed on the List of Mankind Treasures of Five Continents by the World Society.

Mark Sarah and Rob Pavlekovic spent around 3,000 in 2007 to reproduce this magnificent church, which is of great historical and cultural significance.

Pueblito Paisa, Colombia

Despite its look and feel, Pueblito Paisa is a more modern part of the Antioquia Region located on top of Nutibarra Hill above the metropolis of Medellin in Colombia. The original Pueblito Paisa (which means little town) was constructed in 1976-77 and inaugurated on 3 March 1978 by then-Mayor Dr. Guillermo Hipcapie Orozco and then Director of Medellin Tourism, Mrs. Nichols Mariluz Vallejo. Mrs Nichols later became Charge d'affaires for Colombia in Australia and helped construct the model on display at Cockington Green Gardens.

Pueblito Paisa is a replica of a typical turn-of-the-century Antioquia town. It has become very important for locals to escape the hustle and bustle of Medellin and glimpse a birds-eye view of the city below and nearby mountains and valleys. The older look of Pueblito Paisa was greatly assisted by repurposing old material, which was recycled into many of the buildings.

Doug Sarah took around 450 hours to construct the model at Cockington Green Gardens with Mrs Nichols and some of her diplomatic colleagues from various South American countries Isla has picked up the vibrancy of Colombian life through the colourful vehicles occupying space in the courtyard scene.

Isla Patterson

9 781922 603623